7 TIPS TO CRAFT

A

DREAM
HOME

Why Spending Millions Can't Always Guarantee That

7 TIPS TO CRAFT A DREAM HOME

Why Spending Millions Can't Always Guarantee That

Prateek Garg

Worldwide Published by
Pendown Press

PENDOWN PRESS LLP

An ISO 9001 & ISO 14001 Certified Co.,

Regd. Office: 3767A, Kanhaiya Nagar,

Tri Nagar, Delhi-110035

Ph.: 8130886000, 9650072927, 8595249536

E-mail: info@pendownpress.com

Branch Office: 1A/2A, 20, Hari Sadan, Ansari Road,

Daryaganj, New Delhi-110002

Ph.: 011-45794768

Website: PendownPress.com

First Edition: 2024

Price: ₹399/-

ISBN: 978-93-5554-804-7

Layout and Cover Designed by Pendown Graphics Team

Printed and Bound in India by Thomson Press India Ltd.

CONTENTS

ACKNOWLEDGEMENTS

Message From My Heart To My Loved Ones

MUMMA and PAPA, you have always been my biggest supporters and sources of inspiration. Thank you for encouraging me to pursue my passion for interior design and for always reminding me to never give up on my dreams. Your love and encouragement have been invaluable to me, and I couldn't have done this without you.

I would also like to thank my mentors Akshar Sir and Shashank Goel without whom this journey would never have been possible.

This message wouldn't be complete if I didn't take a moment to express my heartfelt gratitude to my wife, Ayushi Garg, for her unwavering support and encouragement throughout the creation of this book.

Her patience, understanding, and unwavering belief in me have been a constant source of strength and inspiration. She has been my sounding board, my editor and my biggest cheerleader, always pushing me to strive for excellence.

I am thankful to my friend Dinesh Verma, CEO, Pendown Press and his team for their support and suggestions throughout the creative process.

INTRODUCTION- SETTING THE CONTEXT

A smart & sustainable home design can work wonders in your life and fill it with love, happiness and prosperity provided you design and execute it in a planned manner.

Trust me, I talk from experience and in the coming chapters I will be sharing all these secrets with you.

Excited??? ....

So am I to help you design and create the home of your dreams exactly the way you envision it....

So, now that I have boldly asked you to trust my experience, you must be eager to know who I am. Ok then let's turn the page & allow me to introduce myself.

MY STORY

Hello My name is Prateek Garg. I am a Home Interiors Expert.

My tryst with home interiors and furniture manufacturing began nearly a decade back.

Ever since then, it has never failed to not only fuel me to establish lasting relationships with my clients but also in terms of building their *"SAPNO KA GHAR (DREAM HOME)"*.

I live and breathe home interiors daily. I am passionate about it & it gives me great joy to add value to people's lives on a consistent basis.

Over the years, I have successfully designed homes & provided furniture to more than 1627 families and helped them create more value and build a home full of love, happiness and prosperity.

The journey so far has been brilliant.

WHY THIS BOOK?

At this point, I'm sure that most of you must be wondering why I am sharing this book with you completely free when I could have charged a premium for sharing this information.

After all, if you implement the suggestions contained within this book, you can easily build the home of your dreams.

Besides, as we are often taught in the business parlance, that "There is no free lunch". Therefore, all the more reason for you to wonder—

Why this free book?

There are 2 reasons behind this free book—

* One is my love for home interiors, it truly breaks my heart to see how people are not able to build their dream homes despite spending so much time and money. So I want to guide the maximum number of people to be able to build their dream home successfully without wasting huge sums of money.

* Two, much as I would love to, I am unable to do all homes personally due to time constraints.

So this book is my gift to homeowners & other designers to share valuable lessons that I have learnt during my journey as an interior designer.

This book & these lessons will function as your professional guide & companion steering you onto the path of building your Dream Home effortlessly and successfully.

The tips that I share are based on certain common design parameters & elements such as the layout, the ceilings, the lighting and other fixtures, wall treatments, vaastu & automation.

Also, apart from the aesthetics and functionality of any home, there is another critical factor that decides the positivity of your home. It is the energy of your home. This energy can be maintained by creating the right flow by aligning with positive elements and forces.

Therefore for every room, I have shared significant vastu tips to help you align the energy in your home towards positivity and harmony.

Additionally, I have shared some bonus Golden Tips that will be true game-changers and will help you design like a pro.

So without further ado, let's explore the

"7 Tips to Craft a Dream Home"

Prateek Garg

#ApkaInteriorWala

#1millionDreamhomes

#The Entrance/Foyer – Where Every Welcome Begins

Elevate Your Home Entrance Experience

The home entrance serves as the gateway to personal sanctuaries, welcoming inhabitants and guests alike into the heart of a dwelling. It sets the tone for the interior ambiance, blending functionality with aesthetic appeal.

Shared below are tips and hacks to help you successfully create and elevate the first checkpoint of your home, the foyer so that the guests & inhabitants both feel they are being welcomed in & welcomed back with a warm loving hug.

1# A Welcoming Layout

The layout of the foyer should prioritize functionality while making a lasting impression. Ensure ample space for guests to enter and move comfortably, with designated areas for hanging coats, storing shoes, and offering a warm greeting. Consider incorporating a stylish console table or entryway bench to add both practicality and visual appeal to the space.

2# An Inviting False Ceiling

Elevate the ambiance of the foyer with an inviting false ceiling design that exudes sophistication and charm. Whether adorned with subtle coves, elegant moldings, or contemporary lighting fixtures, the false ceiling sets the stage for a grand entrance, leaving a lasting impression on visitors.

3# Elegant Wall Treatments

Transform the walls of the foyer into works of art with elegant and tasteful treatments. From textured wallpapers to decorative moldings and accent paint colors, explore various options to create a captivating backdrop that reflects your personal style and sets the tone for the rest of your home.

4# Illumination & Atmosphere

The lighting in this space needs to be a combo of down lights, cob lights or profile lights.

Adding track lights to lean foyers can add a tinge of elegance and a wow factor to the area.

Usually, the lux level of around 200 is maintained in entrance areas.

5# Vastu Harmony

Display happy pictures of the family on the northeast wall of the house.

Choose soft lighting such as scented candles, wall lights or lamps to create a serene atmosphere.

6# Smart Enhancements

Create a docking space for cleaning robots if not today then for future purposes.

Install motion-sensor lighting to illuminate the space automatically as guests enter, integrate a smart doorbell for added security and peace of mind, and consider implementing a home automation system to control lighting, temperature, and security features with ease.

The Golden Tip

Don't clutter the space with too many colors and finishes. If the space is too compact, consider adding mirrors to the area to make the area feel big.

#The Drawing Room - Where Elegance Meets Comfort: Your Stylish Haven for Gatherings and Reflections.

The Drawing room is a space where you cater to your guests and welcome people into your home. A well-designed drawing room will help your guests enjoy the space and feel comfortable.

Use the following tips to create a space that is not only beautiful and unique but also feels like a home to your guests.

1# A Welcoming Layout

The layout of the foyer should prioritize functionality while making a lasting impression. Ensure ample space for guests to enter and move comfortably, with designated areas for hanging coats, storing shoes, and offering a warm greeting. Consider incorporating a stylish console table or entryway bench to add both practicality and visual appeal to the space.

2# An Exquisite False Ceiling

Elevate the ambiance of the drawing room with an exquisite false ceiling design that exudes opulence and refinement. Adorn the ceiling with intricate details and decorative elements, such as coves and ornate moldings, to create a sense of grandeur and sophistication. Incorporate elegant lighting fixtures, such as chandeliers or pendant lights, as focal points to illuminate the space with a warm and inviting glow.

3# Refined Wall Treatments

All walls should have a basic level of designing and one wall should be highlighted to stand out which is usually called the accent wall.

4# Illumination & Ambiance

Aim for a luxuriously comfortable lighting level that enhances the beauty of the space while providing ample illumination for relaxation and entertainment. The lighting in the drawing room should have focus lights with down lights, designer chandeliers and wall pieces. The preferred lux level for the drawing room is between 100-150 which can go down up to 60.

5# Timeless Elegance with Vastu

The seating arrangement is very important to ensure that we promote positive vibes in our home and the guests entering the space should also get carried away with the vibe. Select north-west or south-east directions for seating and maintaining overall peace and relaxation.

6# Combine Modern Luxury with Smart Technology

Embrace modern luxury and convenience in the drawing room by integrating smart technology and innovative features into the design. Install smart lighting controls, automated window treatments, and state-of-the-art entertainment systems to enhance comfort and enjoyment while adding a touch of sophistication to the space.

Install motion-sensor lighting to illuminate the space automatically as guests enter, integrate a smart doorbell for added security and peace of mind, and consider implementing a home automation system to control lighting, temperature, and security features with ease.

The Golden Tip
Infuse the drawing room with personalized touches and cherished heirlooms that reflect your unique tastes and preferences. Display art pieces, family photographs, and treasured mementos that tell the story of your life and experiences, adding warmth and character to the space.

#The Family/Living Room - Crafting Memories, One Elegant Moment at a Time:

The family room is that area of the house which makes the most memories & bonds, and can be termed as the happy place of the house.

It is a place for the family to huddle together in happy and challenging times. It needs to be cheerful, tasteful and functional. A space that can make the happy times happier and challenging times restful yet uplifting.

So go ahead and use these amazing tips to create a space that will truly bring and keep your family together and bonded.

1# An Inviting Layout

The layout of the living room sets the stage for relaxation and connection, with ample seating arranged to accommodate all family members comfortably. Opt for casual, inviting furnishings that encourage relaxation and facilitate meaningful conversations. Consider incorporating a large TV screen or entertainment center to enhance family gatherings and leisure time.

2# An Elegant False Ceiling

Create a sense of sophistication and style with an elegant false ceiling design. Incorporate subtle coves and lighting fixtures to add depth and visual interest to the space, while ensuring a balanced and harmonious ambiance that complements the overall decor.

3# Stylish Wall Treatments

Elevate the aesthetic appeal of the living room with stylish wall treatments that reflect your personal taste and style. From textured wallpapers to decorative wall panels and artful arrangements, infuse the space with character and charm, making it a reflection of your unique personality.

4# Illumination & Ambiance

The living room lights should have an option of down lights and strip/profile lights. Looping should be done in such a way so that we can create multiple lux levels. The Lux level ranges from 50-150 in living rooms usually.

5# Vastu Tips

Bring the aesthetics of nature to your space by adding plants in the north-east corner of your living room. This brings positive vibrations to the living room.

6# Smart Home Integration

Enhance the functionality and convenience of the living room with smart home technology and automation. From voice-controlled lighting and entertainment systems to integrated sound systems and temperature control, harness the power of technology to elevate your living experience and simplify daily routines, chatting, chilling and watching Netflix.

The Golden Tip

Infuse the living room with personal touches and meaningful accents that reflect your family's values, interests, and experiences. Display cherished photographs, artwork, and heirlooms that tell the story of your journey together, creating a warm and inviting space that feels truly like home.

#The Dining room – Where Culinary Delights and Timeless Conversations Unfold

"Step into our dining room, where every meal is a celebration and every conversation is seasoned with warmth. Here, culinary excellence meets timeless elegance, creating a space to savour the joy of shared moments."

Use the wonder tips shared below to create/transform your dining space that motivates and compels your entire family to eat together and is a delicious delight for your guests.

1# An Inviting Layout

The dining room is a space where you dine and discuss your days. Ensure that the dining table should have enough space to accommodate all members of the house & guests. If space permits add a statement crockery unit for designer crockery.

2# A Subtle False Ceiling

The ceiling needs to be planned in a way that the dining table placement falls central to the design or part of it. It shouldn't feel misaligned or unplanned. A nice carpet underneath the table and an art piece on one of the side walls add elegance to the space.

3# Harmonius Wall Treatments

Achieve visual cohesion by harmonizing the main seating wall and any LCD walls with consistent design materials. Embrace the trend of wall trims paired with stylish wallpapers, adding depth and character to the dining room's aesthetic.

4# Illumination & Ambiance

The living room lights should have an option of down lights and strip/profile lights. A lux level of approx 150 which can be adjusted to 100 or 200 as and when needed.

5# Vastu Tips

Ideally, one should eat meals facing east, west or north. Regularly eating meals, while facing south, will invite health issues. The dining table should be square or rectangular in shape and not round or of any irregular shape.

6# Enhanced Technology Integration

The dining room usually has compact spaces so we can make the dining table with a bench which can slide inside the table when the sitting needed is less and pulled out when guests are there. Elevate the dining experience with mood-setting lights and Alexa-operated appliances, allowing families to create the perfect atmosphere for shared meals, relaxation, and entertainment.

Install motion-sensor lighting to illuminate the space automatically as guests enter, integrate a smart doorbell for added security and peace of mind, and consider implementing a home automation system to control lighting, temperature, and security features with ease.

The Golden Tip

A dining room is a place where all family members dine and discuss their day gone by or have fun conversations it is suggested to keep mobile phones away from the table with a no mobiles policy.

#The Kitchen - Where Culinary Creativity Flourishes and Bonds Strengthen

Any kitchen needs to be designed keeping in mind the utilities, requirements and choices of the operator. Each kitchen will be designed on the basis of the family size, operator and the way of dining etc.

If you incorporate or implement the following tips into your kitchen design, I guarantee that your kitchen will look like that featured in a magazine and will be so functional that working there will be a joy for whosoever works there.

1# A Functional Layout

The kitchen needs to accommodate a cooking area, washing area and appliance operating space. You need to ensure a triangle is created between these three and also a proper working space is created in case two or more areas need to be managed simultaneously.

2# A Practical False Ceiling & Electrical Points

The design of the kitchen space doesn't need any funky designs in the ceiling. A simple cove or plain with profile lights will do. While giving electrical points ensure that there are enough 16amp switches to use appliances & switches are accessible easily.

3# Utilitarian Wall Treatments

We need to ensure that to increase woodworking life and stay away from termites we put waste tiles on spaces covered by kitchen structures. Also, get a waterproof putty primer done on the walls.

4# Illumination & Efficiency

The kitchen requires detailed working and focus. So ensure a lux level of 400 on worktops and 150-200 in common areas. Also, make sure you have enough down lights and focus lights to provide the desired illumination levels.

5# Harmonious Vastu

The Lord of Fire—Agni—prevails in the south-east direction of the home, all the objects inside the kitchen represent fire, so gas stoves, cylinders, microwave ovens, toasters, among other appliances should be placed in the south-east part of the kitchen. Also, these items should be placed in a manner which will compel a person to face the east while cooking. This will ensure positive energy in the kitchen as well as the entire house.

6# Innovative Technology & Smart Fittings Integrations

From programmable ovens to touchless faucets and smart refrigerators, integrating modern technology into the kitchen can revolutionize the cooking experience and simplify daily tasks. A rolling shutter is recommended to segregate the space for grinders, mixers etc. It adds to the look and utility of the kitchen space.

The Golden Tip

While putting the marble on the slab put a PVC/ WPC board between the carcass and marble so in case there is any leakage from the top it goes to the waterproof area and not the wooden carcass.

Also, make the sink area without any back ply to ensure all leakages are spotted immediately.

#The Parents' room – A Sanctuary of Love and Comfort: Where Parenthood Finds Peaceful Retreat

Parents' room is the epicenter of peace and calmness. It is important to ensure it has comfort and planning as per their stage of life and where their children and grandchildren can come and sit with them. A dedicated space for their evening tea would be the icing on the cake.

With the tips given below, you can create a serene and uplifting space for your parents and make this a beautiful gesture to reflect back at them the love they have given and continue to give you.

1# A Serene Layout

A parents' room should have a smooth flow with enough moving space around furniture. Avoid using things with sharp corners & edges and provide space to put medications etc in a closed yet accessible space. Also, ensure a sitting space in the room for other family members to come and sit and talk to them or for the couple to relax together.

2# A Restful False Ceiling

Enhance the ambiance of the parents' room with a restful false ceiling design that soothes the senses and promotes relaxation. Choose soft, neutral tones and gentle curves to create a serene and inviting atmosphere, complemented by subtle lighting fixtures that cast a warm and comforting glow.

3# Tranquil Wall Treatments

Embrace tranquil wall treatments that evoke a sense of peace and serenity in the parents' room. Opt for calming colors, such as soft blues, greens, or neutrals, to create a soothing backdrop for rest and relaxation. Consider incorporating textured wallpaper or subtle patterns to add visual interest without overwhelming the space. Do place family portraits and their old pictures on the empty walls. This promotes emotional well-being.

4# Ambient Lighting & Comfort

Illuminate the parents' room with ambient lighting that promotes relaxation and comfort. Install dimmable lights to adjust the mood and ambiance according to preference, whether it be for reading, unwinding, or intimate conversations. Incorporate bedside lamps or wall sconces for soft, diffused lighting that creates a cosy and inviting atmosphere. The lights should be in a warm white tone (2700-3000k) with an ideal range of 60-100 lux level going up to 150 max.

5# Harmonious Balance with Vastu

The East and the South-West directions of the house deal with the good health of the elderly. In case there is a vastu dosha in this direction; their bedroom is not in the proper direction, or there is some vastu defect in the interiors of the room, it directly affects the health, age and relationship of the seniors with the rest of the family members.

6# Smart fittings integrations

A remote to switch on/off the lights will be useful. Alexa-operated lights also help where we can set different moods. Also having sensor lights in the washroom passage will be beneficial for late-night use. Also, a timer in the geyser switch will save the daily hassle of switching on the geyser early morning.

The Golden Tip

I am sure you hear common injuries and falls for the elderly of the house often. The easiest way to reduce the impact is to have wooden flooring as it absorbs the impact of fall and reduces the chance of any injury or fractures due to fall.

Also, ensure anti-skid mats and easy grab bars in the wet areas of their en-suite bathroom.

#The Married Couple's Room/Master Bedroom - A Serene Haven for Two Hearts

Step into your married couple's room, a private retreat designed for intimacy and relaxation. Here, every detail is curated to foster closeness and connection between partners. From cosy furnishings to the soothing ambiance, it's a space where love flourishes and cherished memories are created.

To make this dream of yours come true, follow the tips shared below and you are sure to achieve your vision effortlessly.

1# An Intimate Layout

The layout of the married couples' room is designed to foster closeness and connection between partners. Opt for a cosy and intimate arrangement of furniture, centered around a luxurious bed adorned with soft linens and plush pillows. Create inviting nooks for relaxation and reflection, such as a reading corner or seating area, where couples can unwind and enjoy quiet moments together.

2# A Romantic Ambient Ceiling

Building a false ceiling which has a combo of different lighting with concealed speakers will be beneficial. Also, the room should have points and sockets near the bed for phone/laptop charging.

3# Sensual Wall Treatments

The walls should have modern colors and the ideal combo is to have louvers with wallpapers and art pieces. A perfect blend of these can be used to reflect their choices, preferences and likes. Ensuring a sense of belongingness reflective of their love and shared experiences.

4# Intimate Illumination

Illuminate the space with soft, flattering lighting that enhances the mood and creates a sense of intimacy. Incorporate dimmer switches to control the brightness levels and create a customizable ambiance tailored to each moment shared together. Warm white is the color to choose with a lux level to be managed between 60-100 with a maximum of up to 150.

5# Harmonious Feng Shui (Vastu)

It is only natural that couples (especially newlyweds) would want to place their wedding or pre-wedding pictures in their room. According to Vastu Shastra, pictures should be placed on the eastern wall of the bedroom. This will ensure that understanding prevails in the relationship. The eastern wall boosts positivity.

6# Smart Fittings Integrations

The room should have smart home features like smartphone/Alexa-operated curtains, and lights which are dimmable and tunable with the possibility of setting multiple modes.

The Golden Tip

A bed size of 7 feet wide is recommended to accommodate children for their early morning snuggles or late-night cuddles.

Also having a space beside the bed for a cot or toddler bed would be ideal for current or future needs.

#The Kids' Room –
Where Imagination Soars
and Adventures Begin

Step into the vibrant kids' room, a space designed to inspire creativity and imagination. Here, colorful décor, playful themes, and interactive elements foster endless adventures and learning opportunities. From cosy reading nooks to imaginative play areas, it's a joyful sanctuary where dreams take flight.

And no, this is not a dream or a page from a home decor magazine. This can be your reality easily and effortlessly if you follow the tips shared below in detail.

1# A Playful Layout

The layout of the kids' room should be designed to inspire creativity and play. Incorporate ample floor space for activities and storage solutions that encourage organization and tidiness. Consider versatile furniture pieces, such as bunk beds or loft beds with built-in desks or play areas, to maximize space and functionality while fostering a sense of fun and adventure.

2# Fun Ceilings

The false ceiling for the kids' room is designed as per the theme with stars, moon, flowers, toys etc being the most popular themes. You can carry the bed back theme to the false ceiling as well. For electrical points, you need to ensure that there are proper sockets around the study area.

3# Interactive Wall Treatments

Elevate the kids' room with interactive wall treatments that engage young minds and stimulate creativity. Consider chalkboard or magnetic paint for one wall, allowing children to express themselves freely and display their artwork or create ever-changing masterpieces. Install shelves or cubbies for displaying toys, books, and collectibles, providing opportunities for exploration and discovery.

4# Cheerful Lighting

Illuminate the kids' room with cheerful lighting fixtures that create a warm and inviting atmosphere. Incorporate overhead lighting, task lighting, and nightlights to provide ample illumination for play, reading, and bedtime routines. Choose whimsical light fixtures in playful shapes or designs that add an extra touch of magic to the space. Warm white is the color to choose with a lux level to be managed between 60-100 with a maximum of up to 150.

5# Harmonious Vastu

The most important vastu tip for a kid's room is to ensure that the child's bed is positioned in the south-west or south direction of the room. This placement is believed to promote stability, health, and overall well-being for the child. Additionally, it's essential to avoid placing the bed under overhead beams or sloping ceilings to prevent negative energy accumulation.

6# Smart Fittings Integrations

Integrate a smart speaker for entertainment and educational purposes. Kids can use voice commands to play music, listen to audiobooks, or ask questions for learning.

The Golden Tip

The Kid's room is a space where all the fun happens so ensure that you incorporate a wooden floor for a soft landing for all the falls and conceal the corners to avoid any serious injury.

Using fabrics that are dark and easily washable is advised and walls with washable paint would be ideal to handle their craft work.

#The Mandir/Pooja Room - Where Devotion Meets Tranquility

The Mandir Room is a sacred space within the home, dedicated to fostering spiritual devotion, inner peace, and tranquility.

Use the tips below to create a pure, pristine & pious space that helps you journey inward & connect to the divine power with ease.

1# A Serene Layout

The Mandir Room layout should be designed to inspire a sense of serenity and reverence. Arrange the space to ensure easy access to the altar or deity, with ample room for prayer, meditation, and contemplation. Incorporate comfortable seating or cushions for devotees to sit and immerse themselves in devotion.

2# A Divine False Ceiling

Elevate the spiritual ambiance of the Mandir Room with a divine false ceiling design. Adorn the ceiling with intricate patterns, symbols, or motifs inspired by religious iconography to create a sacred atmosphere. Consider incorporating soft lighting fixtures or LED strips to illuminate the altar and accentuate the divine presence within the room.

3# Sacred Wall Treatments

Enhance the sacredness of the Mandir Room with sacred wall treatments that reflect devotion and reverence. Install wall decals, murals, or religious scriptures to adorn the walls and inspire spiritual contemplation. Consider incorporating shelves or niches to display sacred artifacts, idols, or religious texts, creating a focal point that draws devotees into prayer and meditation.

4# Illumination and Tranquility

Illuminate the Mandir Room with soft, diffused lighting to create a tranquil and meditative atmosphere. Opt for warm-toned LED lights or candles to evoke a sense of peace and serenity within the space. Ensure that the lighting is adjustable to accommodate different rituals, prayers, and meditative practices performed in the room. Warm white is the color to choose with lux level to be managed between 60-100 with a maximum of up to 150.

5# Sacred Energy with Vastu

Infuse the Mandir Room with sacred energy and positive vibrations by incorporating Vastu principles into the design. Position the altar or deity in the northeast corner of the room, facing towards the east or north, to harness the beneficial energies of the cosmos. Ensure that the Mandir Room is kept clean, clutter-free, and well-ventilated to promote spiritual purity and harmony.

6# Spiritual Harmony with Rituals

Foster spiritual harmony and devotion in the Mandir Room by incorporating daily rituals and practices. Establish a routine of lighting incense, offering prayers, and performing aarti to honour the divine presence and deepen your connection to the divine.

The Golden Tip

Personalize the Mandir Room with sacred artifacts, symbols, and images that resonate with your spiritual beliefs and traditions. Encourage family members to participate in religious ceremonies and observe traditions to cultivate a sense of spiritual unity and reverence...

Dedicate time each day for personal prayer, meditation, or reflection to nurture your spiritual well-being and deepen your connection to the divine.

#The Servants' Quarters – Ensuring Comfort and Efficiency in Service

While the drawing room serves as a hub for elegance and leisure, the servants' quarters are essential spaces that ensure the smooth functioning of household operations. It is crucial to prioritize comfort and efficiency in these areas, providing a conducive environment for the dedicated service staff.

The domestic staff plays a crucial role in the smooth functioning of your household and daily life, ensuring that they get proper rest and residence is essential both from a humane and practical perspective.

1# A Practical Layout

The layout of the servants' room should be optimized for functionality and space utilization. Consider furnishing the room with essential amenities such as a comfortable bed, storage cabinets, and a small workstation. Ensure that the layout allows for easy movement and access to necessary utilities.

2# Basic Comforts

While the servants' room may be modest in size, it should still offer basic comforts to support the well-being of the service staff. Provide amenities such as a clean bed with fresh linens, adequate ventilation, and temperature control to ensure a comfortable living environment.

3# Efficient Storage Solutions

Incorporate efficient storage solutions to maximize space and keep the room organized. Install shelves, cabinets, or storage bins to provide designated spaces for personal belongings and supplies, promoting cleanliness and tidiness in the servants' quarters.

4# Functional Lighting

Ensure adequate lighting in the servants' room to facilitate tasks and activities, especially during nighttime hours. Install overhead lights, task lights, or bedside lamps to provide sufficient illumination for reading, working, and navigating the space comfortably.

5# Harmonious Vastu

According to Vastu Shastra, the Servants' room should ideally be located in the south-east corner of the house, away from the main living areas. The room should be well-ventilated and free from clutter, promoting a positive and productive work environment for staff members.

6# Efficient & Smart Amenities

Smart fittings and appliances may be incorporated into the Servants' room to streamline tasks and improve efficiency. From automated cleaning devices to energy-efficient appliances, these amenities help support staff members in their daily responsibilities.

The Golden Tip

Foster open communication and mutual respect between the household members and staff to create a harmonious living environment. Providing regular opportunities for feedback, recognition, and support contributes to a positive work culture and enhances overall satisfaction.

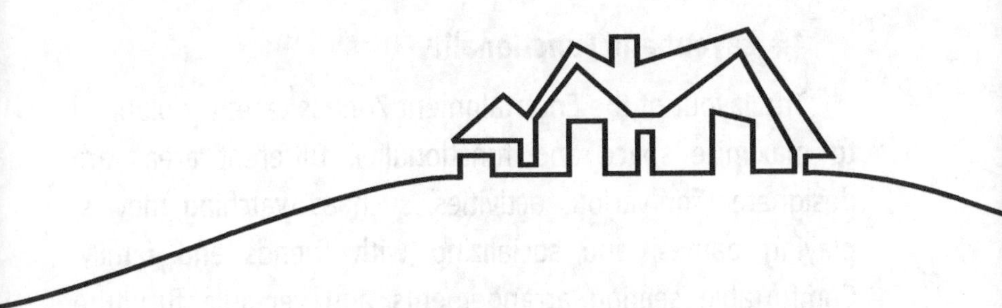

#The Entertainment Zone - Where Fun and Relaxation Meet in Harmony

Step into your Entertainment Zone, a dynamic space designed to delight and entertain. Here, every detail is curated to create an immersive experience where fun, relaxation, and enjoyment reign supreme. From state-of-the-art technology to cosy seating, it's a place where unforgettable memories are made and laughter fills the air.

Follow my tips to create an area where the family can relax, rejuvenate and bond. A space designed to facilitate rest & recreation, a space filled with awesome vibes and great cheer. Create your joy-filled entertainment zone with ease—

1# Layout and Functionality

The layout of the Entertainment Zone is carefully planned to maximize space and functionality. Different areas are designated for various activities, such as watching movies, playing games, and socializing with friends and family. Comfortable seating arrangements and versatile furniture allow for flexibility and adaptability to suit different needs and preferences.

2# State-of-the-Art Technology

Cutting-edge technology takes center stage in the Entertainment Zone, with high-definition screens, surround sound systems, and gaming consoles providing an immersive audiovisual experience. Smart features and home automation capabilities add convenience and ease of use, allowing for seamless integration and control of entertainment devices.

3# Cosy Comfort

Despite its high-tech features, the Entertainment Zone is designed to be a cosy and inviting retreat. Plush sofas, recliners, and bean bags offer comfortable seating options for movie nights or gaming marathons, while soft rugs and throws add warmth and texture to the space.

4# Ambiance and Lighting

Lighting plays a crucial role in setting the mood and ambiance of the Entertainment Zone. Dimmable lights, LED strips, and accent lighting can be adjusted to create the perfect atmosphere for any occasion, whether it's a lively game night or a relaxing movie marathon.

5# Snack Bar and Refreshments

No entertainment zone is complete without a well-stocked snack bar or refreshment station. Mini-fridges, popcorn machines, and beverage coolers ensure that refreshments are always within reach, allowing guests to indulge in their favorite treats without missing a moment of the action.

6# Versatile Entertainment Options

The Entertainment Zone offers a diverse range of entertainment options to cater to different interests and preferences. From movie screenings and gaming tournaments to karaoke nights and board game sessions, there's something for everyone to enjoy.

> ### *The Golden Tip*
>
> *Create a dedicated area for immersive experiences, such as virtual reality gaming or home theater screenings. With the right equipment and setup, guests can be transported to new worlds and enjoy unforgettable adventures from the comfort of your home.*

#Work from Home/Study Room -
A Productive Haven for Focus and Growth

Step into your Work from Home/Study Room, a dedicated space designed to inspire productivity, concentration, and personal growth. Here, every detail is meticulously curated to create an environment where work and study thrive, fostering creativity, innovation, and success.

Using the tips given below create a workspace that will inspire and facilitate focus & productivity with ease and joy.

1# Layout and Ergonomics

The layout of the Work from Home/Study Room is carefully designed to optimize space and promote ergonomic comfort. Adjustable desks, ergonomic chairs, and proper lighting ensure a comfortable and healthy work environment, minimizing fatigue and strain during long hours of work or study.

2# Technology and Connectivity

State-of-the-art technology and reliable connectivity are essential in the Work from Home/Study Room. High-speed internet, efficient workstations, and multifunctional devices enable seamless communication, collaboration, and productivity, allowing occupants to stay connected and focused on their tasks.

3# Organization and Storage

Organization is key in the Work from Home/Study Room, with ample storage solutions provided to keep work materials, books, and supplies neatly organized and easily accessible. Built-in shelves, filing cabinets, and desk organizers help minimize clutter and maximize efficiency, promoting a clear and focused mindset.

4# Inspiring Decor and Motivation

The decor of the Work from Home/Study Room is designed to inspire creativity, motivation, and focus. Inspirational quotes, motivational posters, and artwork that reflect personal interests and goals serve as reminders of the purpose and importance of the work being done, fostering a positive and determined mindset.

5# Quiet and Distraction-Free Environment

Creating a quiet and distraction-free environment is essential for optimal productivity and concentration in the Work from Home/Study Room. Soundproofing measures, noise-cancelling headphones, and privacy screens help minimize distractions and interruptions, allowing occupants to focus on their tasks with undivided attention.

6# Time Management and Productivity Tools

Incorporating time management and productivity tools into the Work from Home/Study Room can help occupants stay organized, focused, and on track with their goals. Calendars, planners, task boards, and digital productivity apps facilitate efficient workflow management and goal attainment, empowering individuals to achieve their full potential.

The Golden Tip

Designate specific work and study zones within the room to create clear boundaries and separate areas for different tasks and activities. By establishing a dedicated workspace, occupants can maintain focus and productivity while minimizing distractions and maintaining a healthy work-life balance.

To Conclude in a Nutshell- Key Takeaways.....................

In conclusion, each chapter presents a unique perspective on designing specific areas of a home, emphasizing the importance of thoughtful planning and attention to detail.

From the welcoming ambiance of the entrance/foyer to the serene sanctuary of the parents' room, and from the vibrant creativity of the kids' room to the tranquil ambiance of the Mandir room, every space is designed to cater to the needs and preferences of its occupants.

The layout, decor, lighting, and Vastu tips are meticulously considered to create harmonious environments that promote comfort, functionality, and well-being. Incorporating smart fittings and appliances adds convenience and efficiency to everyday life, while personalized touches and golden tips offer invaluable insights for creating spaces that truly feel like home.

Whether it's fostering connections in the drawing room, crafting memories in the family/living room, or indulging in culinary delights in the dining room, each space is designed to facilitate meaningful interactions and cherished moments with loved ones.

Furthermore, the dedicated spaces for work, study, entertainment, and spiritual practice reflect the diverse needs and lifestyles of modern households, providing functional havens where productivity, relaxation, and personal growth can thrive.

In essence, these chapters underscore the importance of holistic design principles, where aesthetics, functionality, and emotional well-being converge to create spaces that enrich lives and elevate the human experience within the home.

BONUS CHAPTER

Now that you have reached the end of this book, I have another great surprise for you! This is not the end of the amazing content——-

Here's a BONUS CHAPTER For You with 12 Awesome Checklists that will have you covered in every design aspect of your dream home!

1. STRUCTURAL CHECKLIST

2. ELTECTRICAL CHECKLIST

3. PLASTERING CHECKLIST

4. PLUMBING CHECKLIST

5. PUTTY WORK CHECKLIST

6. PRIMER CHECKLIST

7. CEILING CHECKLIST

8. TILES CHECKLIST

9. 1st COAT CHECKLIST

10. FURNISHING CHECKLIST

11. FINAL COAT CHECKLIST

12. TILE JOINT CHECKLIST

THE WAY FORWARD

Congratulations! Now you are equipped to build the home of your dreams using the 7 tips given for each room. Go ahead— Give shape to your dreams.

However, if you wish to make this process smoother and speedier and derive excellent value for money. If you feel that you need further assistance, get in touch with me for your free consultation and together let's begin the journey toward your dream home......

Whatsapp/Call me - + 91 999 999 4131

Mail me at – Prateek@elatio.in